Environmental Security: Is it a Useful Concept?

SAGHIR IQBAL

ISBN-10: 1725532425
ISBN-13: 978-1725532427

DEDICATION

I dedicate this book to all those who gave me encouragement, support and guidance. Foremost, to my father (late) Raja Mohammed Iqbal and to my mother Azra Begum, from whom I have learnt so much.

CONTENTS

ACKNOWLEDGMENTS

I am very grateful to a host of people for their various contributions towards this book. I am particularly very grateful to Professor Syed Peerzada Mahmud Shah Bookhari who deserves much commendation for his constant encouragement and support throughout the hard times of the programme.

Environmental Security: Is it a Useful Concept?

Members of the Jordanian battalion of the United Nations Stabilization Mission in Haiti carry children through flood waters.

Abstract

Environmental security represents a significant departure from the traditional concept of national security approach to national security. The idea that environmental degradation is a security issue when it is a cause of violent conflict appears to be consistent with the traditional definition of national security. The impact of war and environmental degradation have resulted in many incidents such as, water wells have been polluted, crops torched, forests cut down, soils poisoned, and animals killed to gain military advantage. It is within this context that environmental issues have raised to prominence, and the term 'Environmental Security' has entered the vocabulary of security planners, policy makers and environmentalists.

Abbreviation

ESDI - European Security and Defence Identity

ENVSEC - Environment and Security Initiative

EU - European Union

ESDP - European Security and Defence Policy

NATO – North Atlantic Treaty Organisation

NACC - North Atlantic Cooperation Council

OSCE - Organisation for Security and Cooperation in Europe

UN – United Nations

UNEP - UN Environment Programme

UNDP - UN Development Programme

UNECE - UN Economic Commission for Europe

UK – United Kingdom

USA – United States of America

REC - Regional Environment Center for Central Asia and Eastern Europe

WHO – World Health Organization

Soldiers are helping in the UK floods

Environmental degradation - polution

1 ENVIRONMENTAL SECURITY: INTRODUCTION

Throughout most of the world's history, the variables defining national security have been largely military in nature. Security consisted of the physical defence of the nation, its people and possessions. There has been increasing understanding that factors outside the traditional sphere of military operations have profound effects on the security of nations across the globe. It is within this context that environmental issues have raised to prominence, and the term 'Environmental Security' has entered the vocabulary of security planners, policy makers and environmentalists.

While the term has come into common usage, there is little agreement as to its definition. With the end of the Cold War, traditional concepts of the nature of national security and the methods to achieve it have changed. Bipolar powers had concentrated on traditional national security planning, which had shifted from a strategy of military containment (of the Soviet Union or the USA) to an imperative of (world-wide) engagement employing all the sources of national power. The UN World Commission on Environment and Development (1987) stated the following in regards to security.

"The whole notion of security as traditionally understood – in terms of political and military threats to national sovereignty – must be expanded to include the growing impact of environmental stress – locally, nationally, regionally and globally".[1]

---

[1] NATO Website – issues/science-environmental-security
http://www.nato.int/issues/science-environmental-security/index.html

There are different ways that global environmental problems have been included in the concept of environmental security. This concept has been developed as an alternative to the traditional concept of security, which emphasizes the security of the state and the military means of securing it. The concept of environmental security rises out of a concern that environmental changes and events, especially degradation, are increasingly serious pressures on livelihood security and perhaps contribute to violent conflict.

According to the UN Environment programme, **"More than two billion people have been affected by disasters and conflicts since 2000"**.[2] The impact of war and environmental degradation have resulted in many incidents such as, water wells have been polluted, crops torched, forests cut down, soils poisoned, and animals killed to gain military advantage. This has had a further adverse reactions on the security of the inhabitants of these affected regions.

According to the United Nations Environment Programme (UNEP), **"Over the last 60 years, at least 40 percent of all internal conflicts have been linked to the exploitation of natural resources, whether high-value resources such as timber, diamonds, gold and oil, or scarce resources such as fertile land and water. Conflicts involving natural resources have also been found to be twice as likely to relapse".** The United Nations Environment Assembly on 27 May 2016 had adopted resolution UNEP/EA.2/Res.15 – this was in recognition of managing resources to reduce armed conflict.[3]

This book will look at this non-traditional security aspect and see what impact it has and whether it has been a useful concept. There is widespread evidence that have highlighted potential issues - which could dramatically affect nation states and their security. It has been argued by many that,

---

[2] Disasters and conflicts - https://www.unenvironment.org/explore-topics/disasters-conflicts

[3] International Day for Preventing the Exploitation of the Environment in War and Armed Conflict 6 November – http://www.un.org/en/events/environmentconflictday/

'Environmental Security', gives an impetus to address these issues and find ways to resolve them from another angle.

Background

The demise of the cold war led to re-examination of security issues, the attention to environmental dimensions of security issues has remained high. Concern persists over the possible impacts of global and regional environmental change on social and political institutions and relations within and between states. The argument for an environmental security perspective arose from three key observations:

- environmental threats can have disastrous outcomes,
- traditional security thinking does not prepare nations to deal with these threats,
- and, unlike traditional security issues, environmental threats are not confined by national boundaries.[4]

Common examples of these new threats are climate change and sea level rise, ozone depletion, deforestation, land degradation; over fishing, fresh water scarcity, and increased spread of infectious diseases.[5]

---

[4] Ibid Terry Terriff, Stuart Croft, Lucy James, Patrick M. Morgan, **Security Studies Today**, Polity Press, 1999, p118

[5] Ibid

The definition of international security has been debated extensively by political scientists and others, and has varied over time. Academic discussions of definitions of security significantly expanded to encompass a far wider range of threats to peace, including, particularly, environmental threats associated with the political implications of resource use or pollution. By the mid-1980s, this field of study was becoming known as environmental security. Despite a wide range of semantic and academic debates over terms, it is now widely acknowledged that environmental factors play both direct and indirect roles in both political disputes and violent conflicts.[6]

A Nepalese peacekeeper with the African Union-UN Hybrid Operation in Darfur (UNAMID) plants a tree outside UNAMID Headquarters in El Fasher, Sudan.[7]

---

[6] Richard H.Shultz, Roy Godson, George H. Quester, **Security Studies for the 21st Century**, Brassey's , 1997, p254

[7] International Day for Preventing the Exploitation of the Environment in War and Armed Conflict 6 November – http://www.un.org/en/events/environmentconflictday/

2 THE ENVIRONMENTAL SECURITY CONCEPT

Members of the Jordanian battalion of the United Nations Stabilization Mission in Haiti carry children through flood waters[8]

The Environmental Security Concept

The concept of environmental security was introduced in an attempt to expand this conceptualization of security by suggesting that human-induced environmental degradation and demographic pressures are new emerging security problems at the national and international levels.

Members of the Louisiana National Guard prepare to deploy rescue missions in Texas in the aftermath of Hurricane Harvey in 2017.[9]

The initial work on environmental security argued that environmental degradation will lead increasingly to environmentally based political instability. It is argued that there is a potential that environmental decline may lead directly to violent conflict, but the focus is more oriented towards the notion that the impacts of environmental degradation on nations security is felt in the downward pull on economic performance and, therefore, on political stability.[10]

It is suggested that some forms of environmental change in combination with socio-economic drivers increasingly threaten basic human interests and thus should be considered high order threats to human well-being in the same way a military threat is a high order threat to human wellbeing.

---

[9] Trump Administration Threatens US Environmental Security - http://www.earthisland.org/journal/index.php/elist/eListRead/trump_administration_thre atens_us_environmental_security/

[10] Richard H.Shultz, Roy Godson, George H. Quester, **Security Studies for the 21st Century**, Brassey's , 1997, p254

BP Oil spill blowout

Expanding the concept of Security

Environmental security represents a significant departure from the traditional concept of national security approach to national security. The idea that environmental degradation is a security issue when it is a cause of violent conflict appears to be consistent with the traditional definition of national security.[11]

Some supporters of environmental security consider environmental threats within a structure of national security; others linking environmental problems to non-traditional security concerns encourage the need for a holistic and multidisciplinary approach to global, regional and local environmental problems that threatens the economic well-being of people. According to the academic Dabelko, environmental degradation often undercuts economic potential and human well being which in turn fuels political tensions and conflict.   Whether environmental security is compatible or in conflict with an exclusive focus on the security of the

---

[11] Charles W. Kegley, Eugene R. Wittkopf, **World politics – Trends and Transformation**, St.Martin's Press Inc, 1997, p316

nation-state is a question on which proponents have expressed different views. [12]

From the 1970s onwards, many people started to rethink about security. Lester Brown sought to redefine national security to make the environment a security issue, arguing that the conventional definition of national security should be expanded to include environmental threats resulting from resource scarcity and overpopulation. He examines five major areas of environmental security: energy, biological systems, climate modification, food insecurity, and economic threats to security.[13]

Richard Ullman, written an article in 'Redefining Security' saying that seeks to shift the focus of states away from a definition of security which relies on militaristic aspects alone. He argued for redefining security to include threats other than immediate military ones.[14] Thomas Homer-Dixon, examines different methodological approaches to testing hypotheses of fundamental links between environmental scarcity and social conflict.[15] There are two main arguments commonly presented in favour of rethinking security.

The first asserts that there are threats to state security other than conventional military ones. Non-conventional threats include resource scarcity, human rights abuses, outbreaks of infectious disease and other adverse health problems, population growth, and environmental degradation caused by toxic contamination, ozone depletion, global warming, water pollution, soil degradation, and loss of biodiversity. The second argument professes that 'state' security in itself is a problematic concept that needs to be radically altered. This implies that the so-called non-conventional threats also act at levels other than the state.[16]

---

[12] Ibid
[13] Alan Collins, **Contemporary security Studies**, Oxford University Press, 2007, p186
[14] Ibid
[15]Alan Collins, op cit:188
[16] Ibid

Non-conventional threats:

Resource Scarcity

An Arab Spring with No Water: How Uprisings in the Middle East Can Be Linked to Resource Scarcity[17]

Water scarcity due to drought and poor conservation of water

---

[17] An Arab Spring with No Water: How Uprisings in the Middle East Can Be Linked to Resource Scarcity - http://georgetownsecuritystudiesreview.org/2016/11/13/an-arab-spring-with-no-water-how-uprisings-in-the-middle-east-can-be-linked-to-resource-scarcity/

Human rights abuses

Outbreaks of infectious disease and other adverse health problems

A council worker sprays disinfectant as a deadly outbreak of the plague spreads through cities across Madagascar[18]

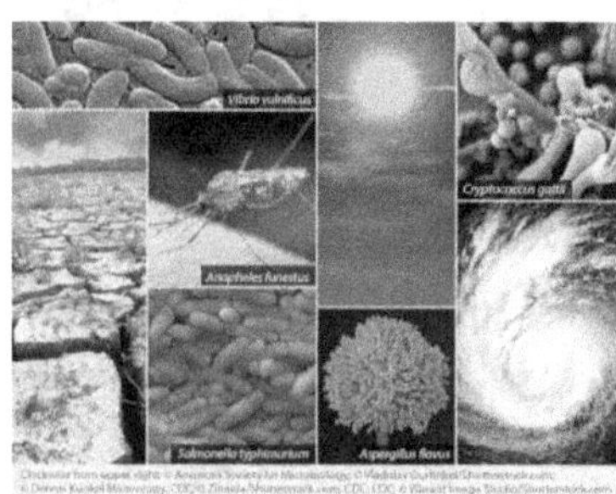

[18]https://www.independent.co.uk/news/health/madagascar-plague-outbreak-mauritius-seychelles-south-africa-who-africa-world-health-organization-a8031591.html

Deadly Ebola virus

Population growth

Global population putting more strain on limited resources

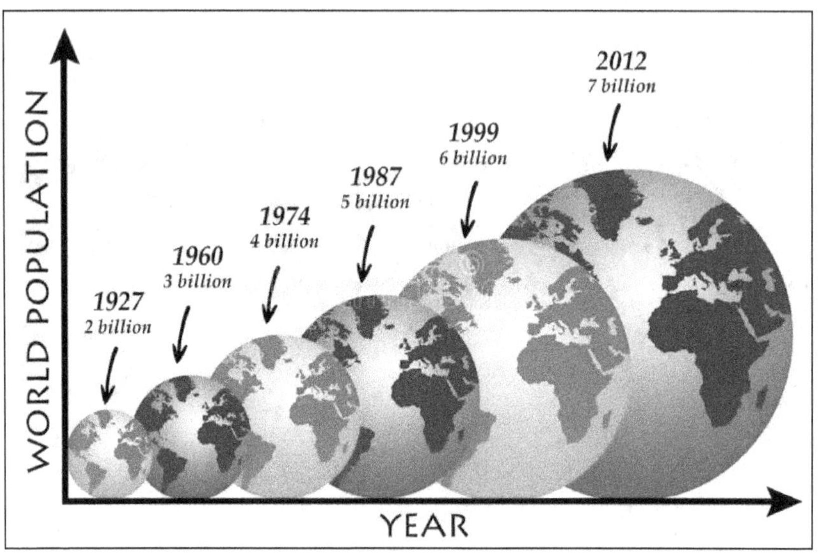

Environmental degradation caused by toxic contamination

Environmental issues are human rights issues[19]

---

[19] Why environmental issues are human rights issues - https://www.business-humanrights.org/issues/environment/why-environmental-issues-are-human-rights-issues

Ozone depletion

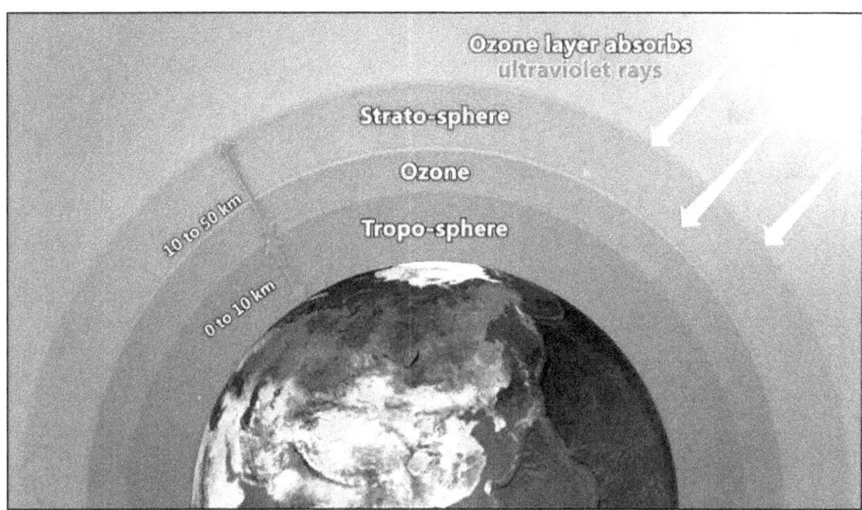

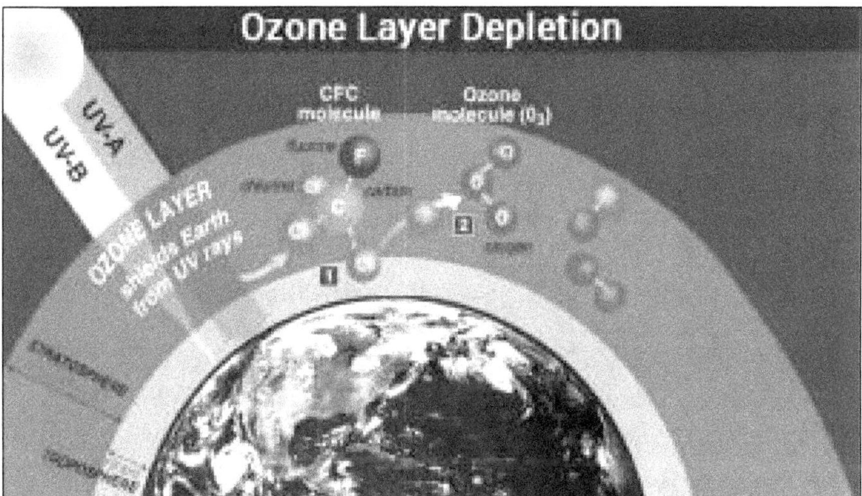

Global Warming

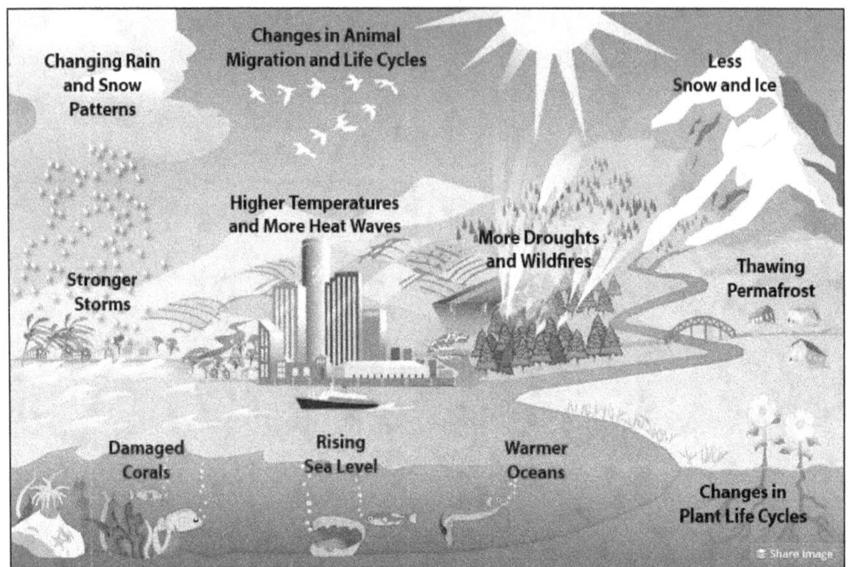
Changing Rain
and Snow
Patterns
Changes in Animal
Migration and Life Cycles
Less
Snow and Ice
Higher Temperatures
and More Heat Waves
More Droughts
and Wildfires
Thawing
Permafrost
Stronger
Storms
Damaged
Corals
Rising
Sea Level
Warmer
Oceans
Changes in
Plant Life Cycles
Share Image

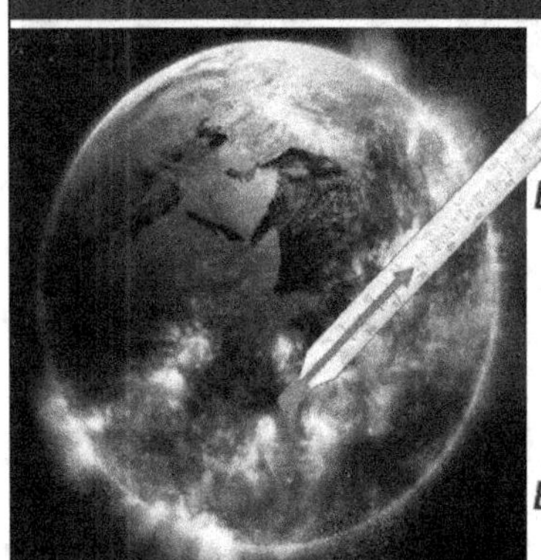
What is Global Warming?
Warmer atmosphere and oceans
Rising sea levels
Changing rainfall patterns
Expansion of deserts in the subtropics
More flooding in coastal areas
Melting of polar ice caps
Melting of glaciers
More extreme weather events
Ocean acidification
Extinction of animal and plant species
Food security threat for humans
The gradual increase in the Earth's temperature caused
by high levels of greenhouse gases in the atmosphere.

Water Pollution

Poluted rivers and oceans

Millions at risk from water pollution

Soil degradation

Loss of biodiversity

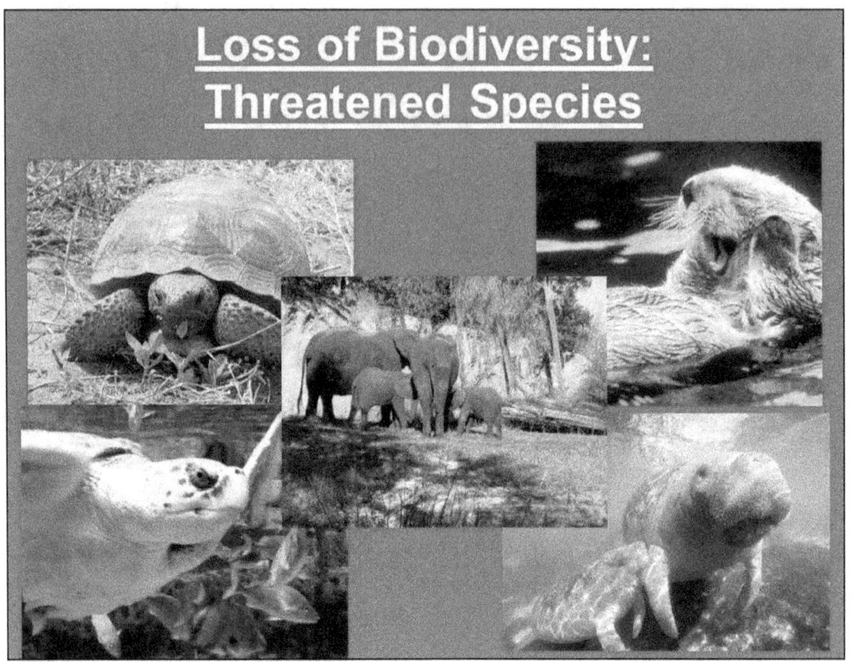

International Cooperation

Environmental security threats often involve trans-border and/or global impacts that would require international cooperation. Nation-states acting alone cannot provide environmental security. International organizations do not have the capability to address the threats. The weight of decision power rests with national governments. As a result, national sovereignty can come in conflict with actions necessary to insure environmental security.

<u>State definitions</u>

There are only few countries that have an official definition of environmental security that unifies thought and action. Among the countries that do have definitions are: Russia, the United States which has several working definitions; China, Australia, and Hungary.[20]

China considers environmental security under the umbrella of 'environmental protection'. Many other countries as well as international

---

[20] Millennium Project Website- Environmental Security Study –

http://www.millennium-project.org/millennium/es-5pol.html

organizations still have doubt about the concept between environment and security. In addition, the relevant international organizations have not created a definition to guide policy. For example the United Nations Environment Program and the World Health Organization (WHO) do not have definitions for environmental security, and the United Nations Development Program only refers to it briefly in its 1994 annual report on human development. Only the collective security alliance - NATO continues to list environmental security as among its most important priorities.[21]

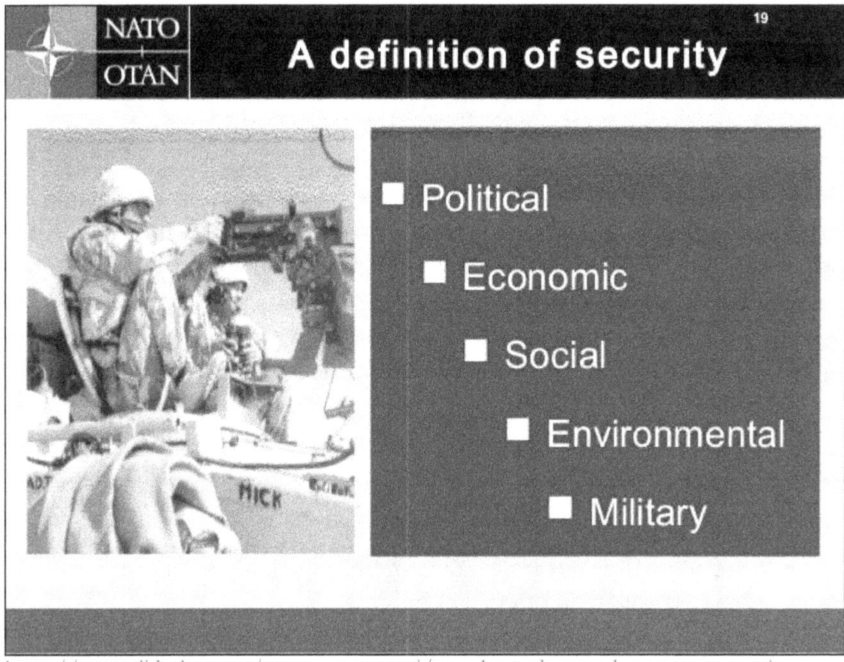

NATO countries have recognised the impact of environmental security and have initiated plans to reduce military activities that have an effect on the environment. The countries in this military alliance intend to respond to the security challenges that have come from the environment.

---

[21] Ibid

NATO troops on exercise

In 1986, it established Committee on the Challenges of Modern Society (CCMS). The committee began to share knowledge on a number of areas in the civilian and military sectors, such as social, health and environmental matters. In 2006, the CCMS had merged with the NATO Science for Peace and Security (SPS) Programme, giving it a wider audience. In addition, this gave an impetus for the establishment of further groups within NATO members that had aim to address the environmental security challenges from a number of positions. It includes two main categories, Environmental Protection and Environmental Security which look into the following activities[22]:

- protecting the environment from damaging effects of military operations;
- promoting environmentally friendly management practices in training areas and during operations;
- adapting military assets to a hostile physical environment;
- preparing for and responding to natural and man-made disasters;
- addressing the impact of climate change;
- educating NATO's officers on all aspects of environmental challenges;
- supporting partner countries in building local capabilities;

---

[22] Environment – NATO's stake (2014) -
https://www.nato.int/cps/cn/natohq/topics_140636.htm?

> - enhancing energy efficiency and fossil fuel independence; and
> - building environmentally friendly infrastructures.[23]

In 2004 NATO had joined with five other international organisation under the Environment and Security programme (ENVSEC). This was primarily setup to coordinate with other agencies its activities that would result in a better impact in its shared vision of environmental security. It was thought that four regions (South East Europe, Eastern Europe, South Caucasus and Central Asia) had environmental issues that could threaten a number of countries security.

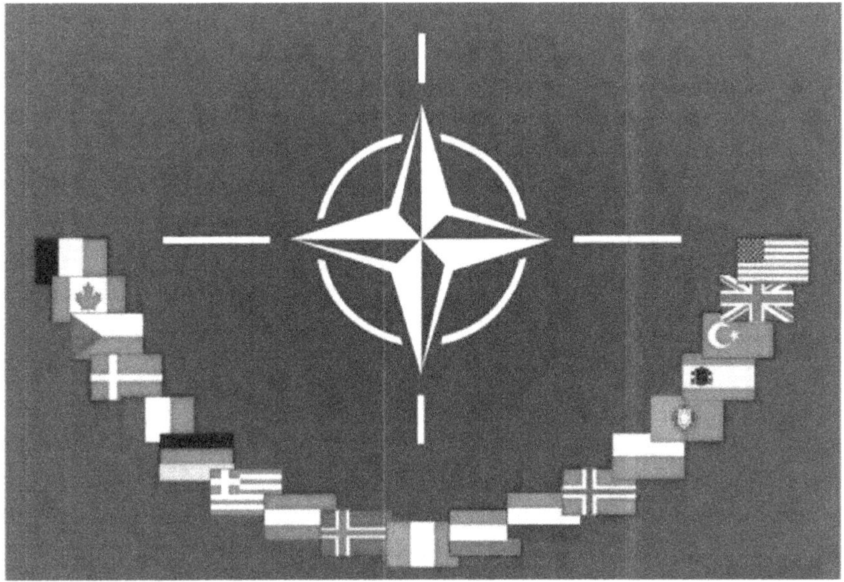

ENVSEC's overall aim is to contribute to the reduction of environment and security risks amongst its partners.

- The Environment and Security Initiative (ENVSEC) is composed of the following partnerships:
- UN Environment Programme (UNEP)
- UN Development Programme (UNDP)

- UN Economic Commission for Europe (UNECE)
- Organisation for Security and Cooperation in Europe (OSCE)
- Regional Environment Center for Central Asia and Eastern Europe (REC)

ENVSEC has helped governments identify common challenges in the field of environment and security since 2003. By 2015, the ENVSEC Initiative has reinforced its thematic concentration amongst many nations.[24] NATO has also been in contact with other organisations, such as the UN and EU to tackle environmental security issues.[25]

In fact, environment and security concerns differ among countries. The developed countries are more likely to be concerned about environment and security in terms of global environment changes and the potential for instability and conflict in strategically important regions of the world. Developing countries on the other hand, with their domestic social and economic challenges, tend to be concerned with the issues of local and regional environmental problems, more from viewpoint of livelihoods.[26]

For instance, the United States has moved officially to redefine national security to encompass environmental threats after the end of the Cold war. Discussion of the links between environment and security has then extended far beyond an academic debate. The US Bush administration was the first to acknowledge environmental security as part of overall U.S (national) security, the Clinton administration has integrated even further in this theme. The article 'failed states' written in 'The Atlantic' by journalist Robert Kaplan was read and discussed among Clinton administration officials.. The article popularized the idea that chaos will emerge as the main threat to global security in future decades. Kaplan declared that population growth and resources depletion would prompt mass migrations and incite group conflicts in Egypt and on the Indian subcontinent.[27]

The former US president Clinton referred to Kaplan's article in describing a

---

[24] Environmental security initiative – https://www.unenvironment.org/explore-topics/disasters-conflicts/what-we-do/risk-reduction/environmental-security-initiative
[25] Ibid

[26] Ibid

[27] Michael Sheeham, **International Security – An Analytical Survey, Lynne Rienner Publishers Inc**, 2005, p100

stark vision of a future world of overpopulated countries, depleted resources, and extreme divisions of wealth and poverty and called for a strategy of 'sustainable development' as a comprehensive approach to the world's future. Also, in the 1994 national security document, the Clinton administration explicitly adopted the concept of environmental security which asserts that increasing competition for dwindling renewable resources is already a very real risk to regional stability around the world. It calls for partnerships between governments and nongovernmental organizations as well as between nations and between regions, and for a strategically focused, long term policy for emerging environmental risks.[28]

According to the Geneva Centre for Security Policy (GCSP), **"The 20th century, as well as the first decade of the 21st century, were marked by grave environmental damage taking place in the course of hostilities. The Paris Agreement and the Global Agenda 2030, among other legal instruments, are a testimony to the increasing awareness of governments and other international actors that environmental issues should be an integral part of addressing larger global challenges".[29]**

The above shows the gradual importance taken by many countries of the importance of environmental security and its implications.

Gold, timber, Ivory plunder – UN Protection

---

[28] Alan Collins, **Contemporary security Studies**, Oxford University Press, 2007, p188
[29] ENVIRONMENT AND SECURITY 2018 -
https://www.gcsp.ch/Courses/Environment-and-Security-2018

3 ENVIRONMENTAL CONCERNS

Resource scarcity

Environmental concerns

In several countries around the developing world, abundant natural resources help fuel conflict, either by attracting predatory groups seeking to control them or by financing wars that were initially caused by other factors. Well-known examples include Sierra Leone, Angola, Democratic Republic of the Congo, Sudan, and Afghanistan. Conflict has also erupted in several countries where the benefits of mining and logging projects—oil in Columbia and Nigeria, timber and natural gas in Indonesia, and copper in Bougainville/Papua New Guinea—build up to a small elite while the social and environmental burdens are borne by local communities.[30]

In addition, resources are not equally distributed, and they are scarce, the relationship between scarce natural resources and international conflict is

---

[30] Joshua S Goldstein, **International Relations**, HarperCollins College Publishers, 1996, p448

controversial. Conflict over the shared waters of international rivers has long been of interest to national security planners. An important example of the relationship between environmental scarcity and water conflict can be seen in the Middle East. The Jordan River basin has often been presented as one of the key examples of where environment and security issues overlap. Jordan River is shared by Jordan, Israel, Syria and Lebanon. Central to the tensions that exist between Israel and the Palestinians is the availability of adequate fresh water supplies. The situation has become so extreme that King Hussein of Jordan singled out water as the only issue that would lead him to go to war with Israel.[31]

Water wars

Potential conflict

---

[31] Ibid

Water conflict

Water has long been considered a security issue in the region, and on numerous occasions, Israel and its neighbouring Arab states have feuded over access to Jordan River waters. In recent times, there was a proposed comprehensive plan for cooperative use of the Jordan River (the Johnston Plan) as early as the 1950s, but this was derailed by the disunity water policy among the four riparian states. Then at the time of the 1967 war, Israel was consuming almost 100 percent of its available fresh water supplies. After the war this situation changed in two ways: 1) it increased the fresh water available to Israel by almost 50%, 2) it gave the country almost total control over the headwaters of the Jordan River and its tributaries, as well as control over the major recharge region for its underground aquifers.[32] The historical factors gave the riparian countries a false impression that war is the only way to escape from the crisis of water scarcity.

Jordan River

Another example of environmental issue leading to international conflict is maritime fisheries. International conflicts over fishing grounds have been frequent in recent decades. Without any international agreement on managing fish stocks that straddle between coastal zone, more than half the world's major maritime fisheries already in serious decline from over fishing and the rest exploited up to or beyond their natural limits, the potential for

---

[32] Ibid

political and even military confrontation is growing. Environment threats in these two cases have intersection with the international security, and it goes far more than traditional competition for control over natural resources.

Nevertheless, war is not the final answer. As the population of the riverside states increase, fresh water supply from Jordan River will become more anxious. Sustainable water-use plans for both states must be well formulated as part of water-sharing agreements, including provisions for greater efficiency in water use by eliminating water subsides, choosing less water intensive crops, reducing water losses in irrigation, minimizing water pollution, and in long terms, population growth as well as migration should be control in a sufferable level. Hence, the primary reason for the decline in maritime fisheries is too many fishing boats with too many fishing technology.[33]

To protect the world's fish stocks from further depletion, the international community will have to establish strict limits on entry into fishing industry; establish binding standards on capitalization of fishing fleets, excessive fleet size, and inappropriate fishing gear; and set a numerical limit on the total catch and the percentage of the total catch per entrant. To enforce such a tough international treaty is to protect a state's interest in continued access to the resources. No military force is utilized in the above approaches, but they are practicable.

---

[33] Sean Kay, **GLOBAL SECURITY in the Twenty- First Century**, Rowman & Littlefield Publishers, 2006, p326

Over fishing are depleting fish stocks

Fishing causing a number of issues

This is what environment security approach offer and it made a clear alternative to traditional conflicts over renewable natural resources. It suggests that the key problem is to conserve the resources in order to maintain adequate supplies well into the future, rather than trying to control more of a resource that is being depleted. In most cases, global agreement is necessary for the resources conservation.

A good example in facing environment threats without using armed forces is the worldwide cooperation in the global warming problems. The Kyoto Protocol was signed by many worlds nation in 1997 within the Framework Convention on Climate Change. It is a success that merely in short time scale the thinning of the stratospheric ozone layer began to slacken and the greenhouse gases reduced. Kyoto is a good case study to persuade other states that international cohesion is effective. Thus, Kyoto provided the evidence that environmental threats could be disentangled by international agreement instead of militarily ways.[34]

---

[34] Peter Hough, **Understanding Global Security**, Routledge, 2004, p146

On a national level, academics such as Bachler and Spillmann stressed that social, political, and economic factors played key causal roles and the environment is usually not a sufficient cause for conflict. This indicates that environment degradation is usually just an indirect cause on violent domestic conflict. Nonetheless it is impossible to ascertain what would happen if the sustainable development been provided early enough. The relationship between environment and violence is interacting in many cases. Environmental and ethnic discrimination come together in ethno-political conflicts either when ethnic groups share a degraded and less productive ecological zone or when a less environmentally advantaged ethnic group moves into the ecological zone of a more environmentally advantaged ethnic group. Centre-periphery conflicts stem from different levels of access and control of environmental services between powerful centre populations and the marginalised periphery.[35]

However, those actions undercut the benefit of the marginal groups whom highly dependent on natural resources for survival could trigger a civil war at any time. For example, in the Kenyan Rift Valley in 1993, violence erupted in the Narok district of Kenya's Rift Valley province. The local Maasai elites, supported by the central government, reacted harshly,

---

[35]Richard H.Shultz, Roy Godson, George H. Quester, Security Studies for the 21st Century, Brassey's , 1997, p260-261

expelling the Kikuyus from a water catchment's area called Enoosopukia. Of course, it could be seen as an environmental excuse for ethnic cleansing in Narok, yet it could also be seen the violence as a by-product of environmental threats.[36]

https://visionvert.wordpress.com/2014/03/17/greenpeace-calls-for-less-talk-more-action-on-global-overfishing

---

[36] Ibid

4 CRITICISMS

Criticisms

All in all, the concept of environmental security has been opposed by some academics, national security specialists, and conservation congressional leaders too. They argued that the terms environmental security:

1)   muddies the concept of security/ drain the terms of its meaning;
2)   result in the militarization of environmental issue;
3)   Was mainly a means of leveraging changes in budgetary allocations;
4)   Environmental issues are not the primary causes of the conflicts.

It has been argued that environmental factors have been increasingly implicated in analyses of development, peace and conflict situations. There is mounting concern over the extent to which environmental stress is threatening livelihoods, health and the fulfilment of basic needs, and harming the sustainability and resilience of fragile ecosystems. Environmental degradation is intensifying conflict and competition over natural resources, aggravating social tensions, and in certain volatile situations, provoking or escalating violence and conflict.[37]

Debate over definition and divergent research agendas

Furthermore, there are concerns among traditional security analysts that the strategy of expanding the security concept to include environmental security will lead to a loss of analytical clarity; security will mean everything and nothing. These concerns have been expressed primarily in academic debate with much contention over the usefulness of environmental security as a concept and on the definition of environmental security.

Some criticisms of the environmental security concept have focused on how the framing of environmental issues as security issues (i.e. 'securitizing' them), potentially affects their handling by governments. Other criticisms focus on the potential for broad definitions of security – including the spectrum from food security to military threats – and make the problem too complex to usefully identify intervention points. A relatively new criticism identified in this review is the failure of conflict focussed studies to address the importance of livelihood security and health as environmentally based issues underlying unrest.[38]

Food security

---

[37] Michael Sheeham, International Security – An Analytical Survey, Lynne Rienner Publishers Inc, 2005, p106

[38] Michael Sheeham, op cit:106-107

Much of this debate then extends towards a discussion of the significance of environmental degradation to people and institutions under different circumstances. It is argued that environmental problems should not be seen as security problems because they are not generally national in character, are not caused intentionally as military threats are, and are more reliably and effectively solved through the development of cooperation than through defensive or offensive military build-up.

There is also disagreement over whether greater understanding of the linkages between environmental degradation and security can be achieved through concentrating efforts on a limited set of cases which result in violent conflict or on the broader set of factors and situations in which environmental degradation creates greater stress on livelihoods without necessarily resulting in conflict.

These problems with thinking about security in relation to environmental threats have a great deal to do with maintaining a distinct research tradition and the practical issue of whether lessons based on organized violence are relevant to managing environmental issues. Daniel Deudney in his essay 'Environment and security: Muddled thinking' argues that environmental problems should not be viewed as security problems because 'traditionally, the concept of national security, as opposed to national interest or well-being, has centred upon organized violence'. He also points out that when an earthquake or hurricane causes extensive damage, it is customary to speak of natural disasters, but not to speak about such events as threatening national security.[39]

This may be true from an American perspective where natural disasters of this type result in largely economic costs, but in a country like Bangladesh where a hurricane can kill thousands upon thousands of people and undermine the proper functioning of economic and social infrastructure the perception may be different, especially for those groups most affected by such events. Ian Rowlands, in his essay, 'The Security Challenges of Global Environmental Change,' presents the counter argument stating: any force that had the power to inflict such harm upon a state—kill some of its citizens and displace others, reduce its agricultural output, threaten its water supply, and destabilize its ecological balance— would be received with considerable attention. He argues that just because these particular challenges are not being issued and controlled by a national leader does not mean that they should be ignored. Indeed, the fact that they are beyond such control makes them all the more threatening and ominous.[40]

Other authors such as Deudney, Waever and Brock for example, suggest that securitizing environmental problems or, in other words, convincing state actors to view environmental problems as security issues could actually legitimise military action to protect state environmental interests. From this perspective 'securitizing' the environment is counterproductive because traditional state security institutions and responses tend not to support the cooperation that is often necessary to adequately address environmental threats. 28 [41]

---

[39] Peter Hough, Understanding Global Security, Routledge, 2004, p148

[40] Ibid

[41] Peter Hough, Understanding Global Security, Routledge, 2004, p148-149

A major part of the justification for a narrower, conflict oriented approach to the environmental security concept has come from the work of Thomas Homer-Dixon who says, "Unfortunately, the environmental-security theme encompasses an almost unmanageable array of sub-issues, especially if we define 'security' broadly to include human, physical, social, and economic well-being." If priorities are not set in the analysis, then the results will not be very helpful to understanding the causes and informing solutions. Instead, Homer-Dixon focuses on the links between environmental scarcity and the extreme situation of violent conflict.[42]

This approach has received a great deal of attention in recent years. It adopts the traditional approach to security as focused on violence especially military type violence, and introduces human-induced environmental degradation as a key driver in causing violent conflict. More recently the notion of human security has been advanced to avoid the narrow focus of the environment and violence approach while at the same time trying to address some of the criticisms levied against an overly broad environmental security concept. Human security focuses on the security of the individual or groups in terms of their well-being.

This approach takes the focus away from state-centred interests and highlights the multiple stresses that may cause insecurity and the types of resilience that promote security for individuals and groups. These authors (such as Dabelko) justify this approach with the following statement: Under certain conditions, such as war, the distribution and composition of force may be the most important determinant of security and insecurity. But in many other situations, security and insecurity will be most closely related to poverty or resource scarcity or social discrimination.[43]

Although this approach does demonstrate that conflict is one aspect among a host of factors influencing individuals' or group's security, it is criticised for its breadth and failing to provide much guidance in identifying which

---

[42] Ibid

[43] Charles W. Kegley, Eugene R. Wittkopf, World politics – Trends and Transformation, St.Martin's Press Inc, 1997, p316

factors to consider or what types of interactions among social and environmental processes are most important.

Increasing polution

Poorer children in the Phillipines – environmental issues

5 CONCLUSION

The concept of environmental security was introduced in an attempt to expand this conceptualization of security by suggesting that human-induced environmental degradation and demographic pressures are new emerging security problems at the national and international levels. The argument for an environmental security perspective arose from three key observations: environmental threats can have catastrophic outcomes, traditional security thinking does not prepare society to deal with these threats, and, unlike traditional security issues, environmental threats are not confined by national boundaries.

On the balance, there is a strong link between environment, conflict and security. And to a large extent, environment is a compact issue of and national/ international security. Even so, there are still many questions and dissents comprise in this topic. How to define environmental security? Should environmental threats under the umbrella of national/international security or should it be a subject on its own? Is the indirect cause like population pressure crucial to resulting violence? Along with the policy-making processes, the major area of disagreement regarded whether policy leadership should come from national governments or international organizations.

Overall, many scholars and practitioners question the operational utility and analytical appropriateness of linking environmental issues with security, raising arguments along the following lines:

(1) Threats to well-being are fundamentally different from military threats;
(2) Overly broad definitions of security render the term useless;
(3) Environmental security is merely another tactic used by developed countries to impose their values on developing countries and infringe upon their sovereignty;
(4) there is a fundamental mismatch between the means required for sustainable development--marked by transparency, cooperation and public participation--and the conflict orientation of security institutions;
(5) Environmental security rhetoric encourages thinking that could lead nations to undertake military intervention in the name of protecting 'global' resources;

(6) Empirical findings that environmental scarcities contribute to violent conflicts are questionable, as environmental factors are at best tangentially related to conflict and in any case are overshadowed by more important socio-political and economic variables.[44]

However, at the very least, the concept of 'Environmental Security' has led to considerable research that has sparked an academic debate and placed environment and conflict on the political agenda. There is also a shortage of skilled and motivated people who fully understand the complex issues involved and their inter-linkages; and can define and manage the necessary actions to reduce the threats to peace arising from environmental degradation and growing competition for resources.

Therefore the usefulness of this concept is essential in that it has highlighted the issues concerned. It has initiated a debate on a global level on the causes of insecurity and the means to learn methods on reducing insecurity by addressing the issues raised in the concept of 'Environmental Security'.

---

[44] Peter Hough, op cit:151

Environmental security and sustainability

Modern technology used to improve better ways of producing food

Reference

Alan Collins, (2007). Contemporary security Studies, Oxford University Press.

Charles W. Kegley, Eugene R. Wittkopf, (1997). World politics – Trends and Transformation, St.Martin's Press Inc.

Joshua S Goldstein, (1996). International Relations, HarperCollins College Publishers.

Michael Sheeham, (2005). International Security – An Analytical Survey, Lynne Rienner Publishers Inc

Millennium Project Website- Environmental Security Study - http://www.millennium-project.org/millennium/es-5pol.html

NATO Website – issues/science-environmental-security http://www.nato.int/issues/science-environmental-security/index.html

Peter Hough, (2004). Understanding Global Security, Routledge.

Philippe Le Billon, (2005). Fuelling War: Natural Resources and armed conflict, Routledge.

Richard H.Shultz, Roy Godson, George H. Quester, (1997). Security Studies for the 21st Century, Brassey's.

Sean Kay, (2006). Global Security in the Twenty- First Century, Rowman & Littlefield Publishers.

Terry Terriff, Stuart Croft, Lucy James, Patrick M. Morgan, Security Studies Today, Polity Press, 1999

Index

Recently released books (2018)

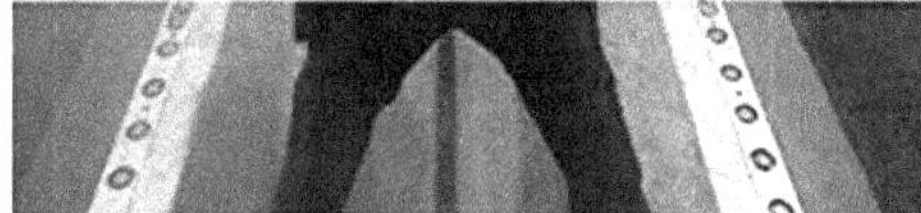

DANGEROUS FLASHPOINTS IN EAST ASIA: THE MILITARY BUILD-UP 2018

SAGHIR IQBAL

Major changes in East Asia have placed the region near the top of the World's strategic agenda. East Asia has until recently experienced the fastest regional economic growth rate in the world for many years. Economic co-operation has been flourishing and economic interests have become the major reason in reshaping East Asian international relations. However, there have also been changes in the security environment, due to many factors, such as the reduction of US forces in East Asia, the disintegration of the Soviet Union (the decline of the Soviet Union's presence in the region had led to renewed attention to traditional and potential rivalries among the major East Asian powers), and the concern of China's hegemonistic ambitions.

Product details

- **Paperback:** 106 pages
- **Publisher:** CreateSpace Independent Publishing Platform; 1 edition (16 Jan. 2018)
- **Language:** English
- **ISBN-10:** 1974062309
- **ISBN-13:** 978-1974062300
- **Product Dimensions:** 21.6 x 0.6 x 27.9 cm

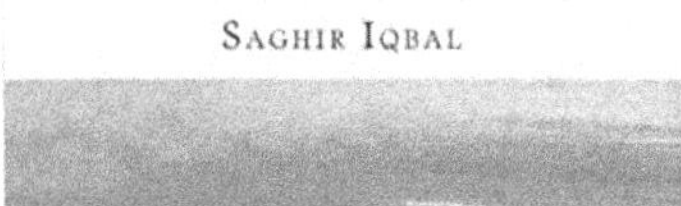

The astronomical rising costs of modern combat has resulted in many countries being deprived of purchasing a modern combat aircraft and this has had an adverse effect on their security. Many nations have tried to undertake cost-effective measures for their defence needs.

Countries can either purchase very expensive modern aircraft or buy older aircraft that can be expensive to operate due to their high maintenance requirements. The Pakistan Air Force had initiated the plan to co-develop an affordable modern multi-role fighter aircraft with China. Chengdu Aircraft Corporation (CAC) in collaboration with Pakistan Aeronautical Complex (PAC, Kamra) have jointly developed the JF-17 Thunder combat aircraft (also known as the FC-1 Xiaolong Fierce Dragon in China).

JF-17 Thunder is a sophisticated light-weight multi-role, all weather, day/night fighter aircraft that is manufactured by Pakistan and China. The JF-17 Thunder has become a very cost-effective aircraft that costs very little compared to other modern aircraft. Many countries have shown an interest and a few have started to make orders. Some have described the JF-17 as the 'Ultimate MiG-21' arguing that the Chinese/Pakistani JF-17 builds on a classic warplane – although it has no resemblance and its level of sophistication is comparable to current advanced fighter aircraft on the market. This very modern and capable aircraft has the potential to become a potent platform that can serve with numerous air forces across the world. Product details

- **Paperback:** 178 pages
- **Publisher:** CreateSpace Independent Publishing Platform (26 Feb. 2018)
- **Language:** English
- **ISBN-10:** 1984055240
- **ISBN-13:** 978-1984055248
- **Product Dimensions:** 21.6 x 1.1 x 27.9 cm

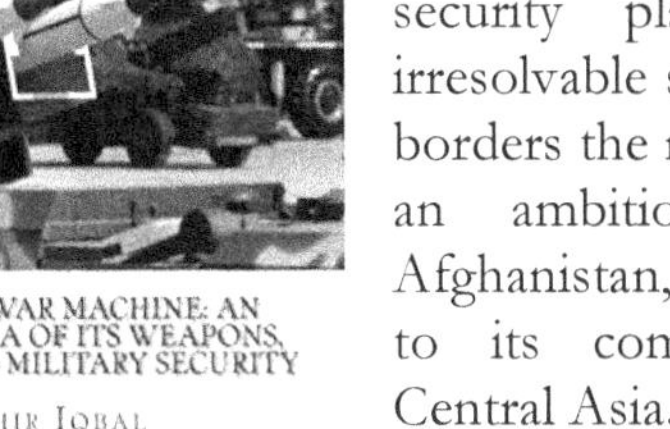

PAKISTAN'S WAR MACHINE: AN
ENCYCLOPEDIA OF ITS WEAPONS,
STRATEGY AND MILITARY SECURITY

SAGHIR IQBAL

The global security challenges after the post-Cold war period has affected many countries. Pakistan's geography and location present its security planners with serious, almost irresolvable strategic and tactical problems. It borders the nuclear states of India and China, an ambitious Iran, and an unstable Afghanistan, which is perceived as a gateway to its commercial-strategic ambitions in Central Asia.

Pakistan's key security problems are a reflection of its history and domestic circumstances. The overriding concern of Pakistan is its internal and external security. Strategically, Pakistan lacks territorial depth. Its main cities and communication routes are relatively close to the border with India and are susceptible to attack. In addition, the headwaters of Pakistan's rivers and main irrigation systems originate from India. Pakistan's borders with India were also new and mainly unfortified and, in many places, were drawn in ways that made them indefensible. Because the borders were also un-demarcated, there was abundant chance for conflict. Pakistan has particularly been affected with a number of issues.

It has been argued by many that a Fourth generation/Hybrid war has been imposed on Pakistan, in order to break the nation (Balkanization of Pakistan into different parts) with the aim of making it either extremely weak or total destruction as a nation state (so that it is not able to challenge the hegemonistic ambitions of its adversaries).The purpose of this book is to assess the military security problems that Pakistan faces, and focus on its external security matters (military threats from neighbouring countries such as India, balance of power in the region, nuclear and ballistic missile threats, relationship with external powers, the high risk of war and its role on the 'War on Terror'), and its internal security problems (sectarianism, proliferation of small arms, refugees, ethnic violence, drug problem, economic weaknesses), and also its ability to cope with these problems.
Product details

- **Paperback:** 366 pages
- **Publisher:** CreateSpace Independent Publishing Platform; 1 edition (13 April 2018)
- **Language:** English
- **ISBN-10:** 1986169421
- **ISBN-13:** 978-1986169424
- **Product Dimensions:** 21.6 x 2.2 x 27.9 cm

MISCALCULATION: RISKS OF
INADVERTENT NUCLEAR WAR

Saghir Iqbal

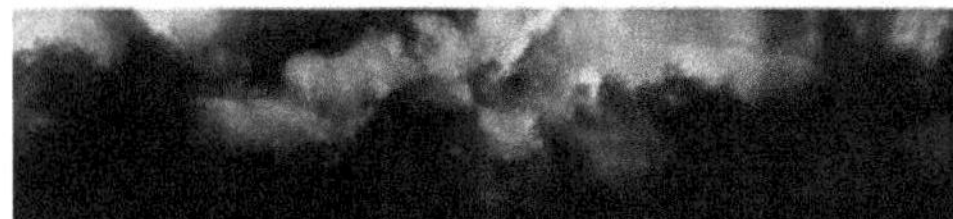

An impending nuclear holocaust is likely to happen, if the world community does not take action. A conflict that has been simmering for many years is beginning to spiral out of control. Two nuclear powers have an unresolved dispute that has increased tensions in the region.

Both countries are purchasing and developing sophisticated state-of-the-art weapons that could unleash great terror and destruction on the populations of both countries – with also serious global ramifications.

The world's most dangerous flashpoint, has the highest chance of a nuclear war occurring – it is deemed by many to be more serious that the Cuban Missile Crisis and North Korea's nuclear sabre rattling. The dispute needs to be amicably resolved between both nations and confidence building measures need to be implemented.

Product details

- **Paperback:** 154 pages
- **Publisher:** CreateSpace Independent Publishing Platform; 1 edition (16 April 2018)
- **Language:** English
- **ISBN-10:** 1717040403
- **ISBN-13:** 978-1717040404
- **Product Dimensions:** 21.6 x 0.9 x 27.9 cm

Pakistan faces a number of threats from internal and external forces – with the aim of weakening the country and an attempt to 'balkanise' Pakistan in to different parts. The Pakistani Chief of Army, General Qamar Javed Bajwa has said that "a hybrid war had been imposed on Pakistan to internally weaken it, but noted that the enemies were failing to divide the country on the basis of ethnicity and other identities".

Furthermore he states, "Our enemies know that they cannot beat us fair and square and have thus subjected us to a cruel, evil and protracted hybrid war. They are trying to weaken our resolve by weakening us from within". Conflicts in Ukraine, Israel and Lebanon (Hizbullah), Syria, Libya, War on Terror in Afghanistan and its impact in Pakistan etc., have resulted in multi-layered efforts to destabilise a functioning state and polarize its society. The centre of gravity is to target population in hybrid warfare. The aim of the adversary is to influence influential policy makers and key decision makers by combining kinetic operations with subversive efforts. The aggressor often resorts to covert actions, to avoid attribution or retribution. At the moment there is no universally accepted definition of hybrid wars – the term is too abstract and is seen by some as using a fancy term to refer to irregular methods to counter conventionally stronger forces.

Accordingly, many say that the new definitions of 4th generation or hybrid wars are really the repackaging of the traditional clash between the armed forces of nation states and the non-state insurgents. This book will be assessing Pakistan's insecurity and the hybrid wars imposed onto it by its adversaries. It will look at a number of issues that Pakistan is facing (military imbalance, economic and political weaknesses, internal and external security threats and the impact of hybrid warfare on Pakistan).

Product details
- **Paperback:** 132 pages
- **Publisher:** CreateSpace Independent Publishing Platform; 1 edition (17 Jun. 2018)
- **Language:** English
- **ISBN-10:** 1721510095

- **ISBN-13:** 978-1721510092
- **Product Dimensions:** 21.6 x 0.8 x 27.9 cm

Each year billions of dollars' worth of arms are procured between various nations, despite the fact that many millions of people live in desperate poverty, many will die from hunger and hunger related diseases. Weapons of increasing firepower and the missiles to deliver them accurately are being acquired, mainly through the Global Arms Trade. This means that we must expect wars in the world to become increasingly violent and destructive.

This book focuses on what the arms trade is and its impact on the world, the wars which have resulted or were sustained by this trade. It is necessary to know which countries sell arms and which ones buy. Also it is important to have some idea of how large the trade is. The international trade in arms has considerably increased since World War 2. Major weapons (aircraft, missiles, tanks and ships) probably account for about one-half of the total trade in weapons and equipment. Many countries and their respective Military-Industrial Complex are 'making a killing' in the world's largest trade in the buying and selling of military technology (weapons).

Product details

- **Paperback:** 90 pages
- **Publisher:** CreateSpace Independent Publishing Platform (28 July 2018)
- **Language:** English
- **ISBN-10:** 1721773150
- **ISBN-13:** 978-1721773152
- **Product Dimensions:** 15.2 x 0.5 x 22.9 cm

The global security challenges since World War II and thereafter (post-Cold war period) has affected many countries. This has resulted in a number of countries pursuing a nuclear weapons programme to provide them with the ultimate security – the belief that the fear of utter annihilation of their opponents would result in deterrence and eventually detente. According to Kristensen and Norris (2014), there are approximately 16,300 nuclear weapons located at some 97 sites in 14 countries. Many of these weapons are in military arsenals (roughly 10,000), with the remaining ones being in the process of retirement and awaiting dismantlement. Accordingly, 93% of the total global inventory resides in Russia and the United States of America. The remaining weapon stockpiles are in the United Kingdom (UK), France, China, India, Pakistan, North Korea and Israel.

This book looks at the proliferation of weapons of mass destruction (WMD), the double standards and hypocrisy practiced by the five declared nuclear powers. It gives a brief short history of nuclear development in the nuclear countries and the impact of nuclear war. It argues that the only way to eradicate these horrendous weapons is for the five declared nuclear powers to make immediate measures to dismantle the weapons and stockpiles of weaponised materials – as they had agreed under the Nuclear Non-proliferation Treaty (NPT).

Product details

- **Paperback:** 146 pages
- **Publisher:** CreateSpace Independent Publishing Platform (31 July 2018)
- **Language:** English
- **ISBN-10:** 1983910414
- **ISBN-13:** 978-1983910418
- **Product Dimensions:** 15.2 x 0.8 x 22.9 cm

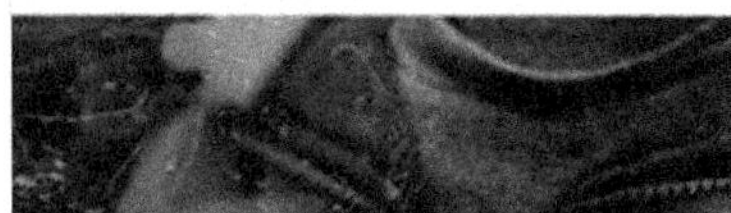

This book looks at the concept of 'terrorism' and its primary aim of creating a climate of fear. Any discussion of terrorism has to firstly define its terms: what do we mean by terrorism and how does it manifest itself in contemporary accounts and moreover, what is the difference between legitimate military action and one based on terror? The definitions of terrorism are complex and depend, to a very large extent, on who one is asking. A government defence adviser would, for instance, have a markedly different notion of what constitutes terrorism than a member of a paramilitary organisation and an ordinary member of the public might have a notion based somewhere on the interaction between these two depending on their socio-cultural background. This is primarily the main reason why the term has not been universally accepted by all scholars or academics.

There are many reasons why political groups attempt to bring about radical change through terrorism. People are often frustrated with their position in society. They may in some way feel persecuted or oppressed because of their race, religion, or they feel exploited by a government. Any group that uses terrorist actions have very complex and powerful reasons to engage in those activities. The usual experience of violence by a stronger party has historically turned victims into terrorists. State terror very often breeds collective terror. Because 'terrorism' is a word that has been used so much and so loosely that it has lost a clear meaning. It can be argued that terrorists are not born, but created as issues of today develop into the conflicts of tomorrow.

Product details

- **Paperback:** 202 pages
- **Publisher:** CreateSpace Independent Publishing Platform (7 Aug. 2018)
- **Language:** English
- **ISBN-10:** 1724714856
- **ISBN-13:** 978-1724714855
- **Product Dimensions:** 15.2 x 1.2 x 22.9 cm

When NATO was founded in 1949, it had a clearly defined role. The demise of the Cold War, the disintegration of the Soviet Union and the collapse of communism in the period from 1989 to 1991 called into question NATO's future role and its continued existence. The primary role was called into question over its future relevance in the post-Cold War world. The reason for NATO was essentially a military alliance to deter Soviet and Warsaw Pact aggression – however, once the threat had finished its role had been challenged by many academics and governments. Many analysts felt that NATO was nothing more than an out of date alliance from the Cold War with no real future. Others would say, however, that an organisation such as NATO was still crucial in the modern world to ensure that countries do not act unilaterally, but co-operate with allies. In view of the situations, NATO has managed to address new issues and adapt its roles on different levels.

- **Paperback:** 66 pages
- **Publisher:** CreateSpace Independent Publishing Platform (10 Aug. 2018)
- **Language:** English
- **ISBN-10:** 1725092816
- **ISBN-13:** 978-1725092815
- **Product Dimensions:** 15.2 x 0.4 x 22.9 cm

ABOUT THE AUTHOR

Saghir Iqbal is a researcher in International Relations and Security Studies. He is an experienced Intelligence Analyst and has achieved a number of qualifications in this field. He is also a Lecturer in Business Management as well as an Examiner for A Level History and Business. Saghir Iqbal has a subject specialism in the following areas:

International Politics of the Cold War 1945-1991
Conflict Resolution in International Society+
Global and North-South Security Studies
Britain in the World
Disarmament Processes: History and Theory
Nationalism and Ethnicity in Post-Cold War Politics
Middle East: Area in Conflict
European Security
International Politics of the Environment
The United Nations, Peacekeeping and Intervention
Disarmament Processes: Current Problems
Globalisation and the South
International Terrorism
International Politics and Security Studies
Introduction to Peace Studies
Politics of the Global Environment
Regional Security in East Asia
Critical Security studies

Recently released books (2018)

- Dangerous Flashpoints in East Asia: The Military Build-up
- JF-17 Thunder: The Making of a Modern Cost- effective Multi-role Combat Aircraft
- Pakistan's War Machine: An Encyclopedia of its Weapons, Strategy and Military Security
- Miscalculation: Risks of Inadvertent Nuclear War
- Hybrid Warfare and its Impact on Pakistan's Security
- Making a Killing: The Scourge of the Global Arms Trade
- Nuclear Apartheid: Bullying, Hypocrisy and the Double Standards on Nuclear Weapons
- Terrorism: Creating a Climate of Fear

Website: www.saghir.co.uk